A YEAR OF FESTIVALS

Christian Festivals

Honor Head

Explore the world with **Popcorn -** your complete first non-fiction library.

Look out for more titles in the Popcorn range. All books have the same format of simple text and striking images. Text is carefully matched to the pictures to help readers to identify and understand key vocabulary.
www.waylandbooks.co.uk/popcorn

First published in paperback in 2012
Copyright © Wayland 2012

Wayland
Hachette Children's Books
338 Euston Road
London NW1 3BH

Wayland Australia
Level 17/207 Kent Street
Sydney NSW 2000

Produced for Wayland by
White-Thomson Publishing Ltd
www.wtpub.co.uk
+44 (0)843 208 7460

Editor: Jean Coppendale
Designer: Amy Sparks
Craft artwork: Malcolm Couch
Picture researcher: Georgia Amson-Bradshaw
Christianity consultant: Reverend Naomi Nixon
Series consultant: Kate Ruttle
Design concept: Paul Cherrill

British Library Cataloging in Publication Data
Honor Head
    Christian festivals -- (A year of festivals)(Popcorn)
    1. Fasts and feasts -- Juvenile literature.
    2. Rites and ceremonies -- Juvenile literature.
    I. Title II. Series
    263.9-dc22

ISBN: 978 0 7502 6970 4

Printed and bound in China

10 9 8 7 6 5 4

Wayland is a division of Hachette Children's Books, an Hachette UK company.
www.hachette.co.uk

Picture Credits: Alamy: Paul Rapson 7; Alex Segre 17; Chris Fairclough: 12; Corbis: Ariel Skelley 4; Eric Audras/ Onoky 8; Stephanie Maze 9; Ricrado Suarez/Epa 10; Gustavo Amador/Epa 11; Dreamstime: Marjanneke 1/15; Lana Langlois 13; Monkey Business Images 14; Marjanneke 15; Airi Pung 21; Photolibrary: Helmut Meyer Zur Capellen 18; Robert Young 2/16; Morgan Lane Photography Front Cover/6; Poznyakov 19; Fotogiunta 20

✝ Contents

Birth of Jesus

Christmas is when Christians celebrate the birth of Jesus Christ. He was born to Mary and Joseph. Christians believe Jesus is the Son of God.

Some children take part in a nativity play at Christmas time, when they act out the birth of Jesus.

Three wise men

Jesus was born in a stable in the town of Bethlehem. He was visited by three wise men, who gave him gifts. Shepherds also came to see him.

Mary

Jesus

Joseph

Shepherd

Happy Christmas!

At Christmas time, many people put up decorations and Christmas trees. Friends and family give each other cards and presents.

Families open their Christmas presents on Christmas Day morning.

There are special Christmas services in the church. People listen to the story of how Jesus was born.

Many Christians sing special songs called carols at Christmas.

Candles remind people of the light Jesus brought into the world.

 # Lent

Lent begins in February and lasts for 40 days. In the past, Christians used to fast during Lent. They would use up all their milk, eggs, butter and sugar before Lent by making pancakes.

Shrove Tuesday, or Pancake Day, is the day before Lent begins.

Many people give up treats, such as sweets and chocolates for Lent.

Some countries celebrate the coming of Lent by having a big street party or carnival. People sing and dance and there is a big parade.

This colourful parade before Lent is in Brazil in South America.

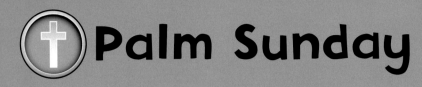 Palm Sunday

Palm Sunday is the beginning of Holy Week. On this day, Christians remember when Jesus rode into Jerusalem on a donkey. His followers cheered and waved palm leaves to welcome him.

In Spain, some children carry palms to church on Palm Sunday.

Many countries have parades on Palm Sunday. Christians walk through the streets to church, singing hymns in praise of God.

In some street parades, Christians carry statues of Jesus and Mary to the church.

✝ Good Friday

Good Friday is the beginning of Easter.
It is the day Jesus was killed by being
crucified on a cross.

The cross has become
an important symbol
for Christians.

People eat special foods at Easter.
Christians in some countries eat
a fruit cake called Simnel cake
and hot cross buns.

Hot cross buns have a cross on top
and are eaten on Good Friday.

Easter Sunday

This is the day that Christians believe Jesus came back from the dead. Many Christians go to church to sing and pray to God.

Christian families share a meal to celebrate Jesus coming back to life.

Easter also marks the beginning of spring and new life in nature. Lots of people give each other Easter eggs to celebrate new beginnings.

Easter is at the end of Lent.

Children paint eggs to give to their family and friends.

Pentecost

Pentecost is important to Christians because this was the time when God sent the Holy Spirit to Jesus's disciples. The Holy Spirit is the power of God.

The white dove is a symbol of the Holy Spirit.

Pentecost takes place about 50 days after Easter.

The power of God helped the disciples as they travelled from place to place. They told lots of people about Jesus and his teachings.

In church, people sing and say prayers to remember Pentecost.

Harvest festival

This is a time in autumn when Christians thank God for the harvest and the food they have. People decorate their church with flowers, fresh fruit and vegetables.

After the harvest festival service the food is given to the poor and elderly.

Many schools celebrate harvest festival. The children have special activities during the day such as making dolls from straw.

Many children bring food to school for the harvest festival.

 Saints' Days

Saints are Christians who have lived holy lives. Saints have their own special days, like a birthday. Some countries have their own saint, called a patron saint.

St George is the patron saint of England.

20

Some countries have a festival to celebrate the special day of their patron saint. Lots of people dress up and there are street parades.

In Ireland, children dress up to celebrate St Patrick's Day.

A patron saint watches over a certain country and the people who live there.

Make a Christmas star

Make a pretty Christmas star
to hang from a Christmas tree or
to use as a Christmas decoration.

You will need:
· Pencil
· Tracing paper
· A large piece of stiff paper or card
· Glitter or stickers for decoration
· Safety scissors
· Thin ribbon or string

1. Cut the card into two squares,
each 10 cm x 10 cm.
Using tracing paper, trace this star
onto each piece of card.

2. Cut out the star shapes.
Cut through each star as shown.

3. Decorate your stars
with glitter or stickers.

4. Slide the two stars
into each other.

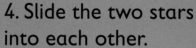

5. Make a hole in the top
of your star and use thread
or ribbon to tie it to your
Christmas tree.

Glossary

crucified how Jesus was killed by being nailed to a wooden cross

disciples these were the 12 men chosen by Jesus to be his close friends and followers

fast a time when someone does not eat or drink anything

harvest the time of year when people gather in all the food they have grown

Holy Week the seven days before Easter

hymns songs that are sung to thank or praise God

nativity birth, especially the birth of Jesus

wise men the very rich men who travelled to see Jesus when he was a baby and brought him presents

Index